Toddler Coloring Book

Picture & Word Coloring Book in Spanish
and English Perfect for Beginners

© 2018 Gurukid
All Rights Reserved

One

Uno

Two

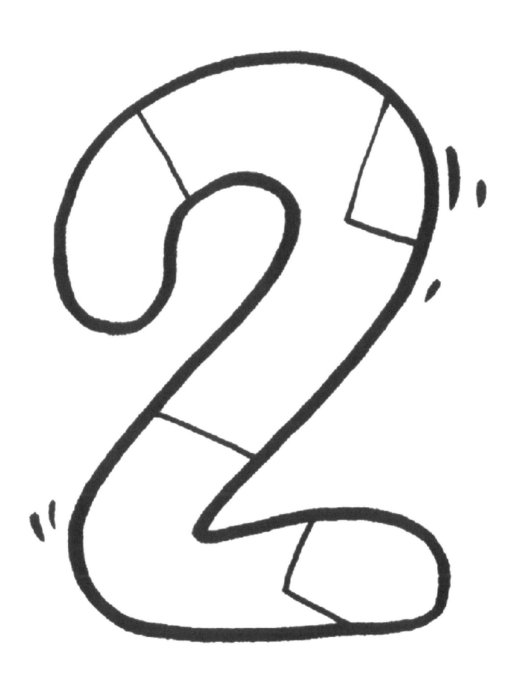

Dos

Three

Tres

Four

Cuatro

Five

Cinco

Six

Seis

Seven

Siete

Eight

Ocho

Nine

Nueve

Ten

Diez

Orange

Naranja

Apple

Manzana

Banana

Plátano

Carrot

Zanahoria

Grapes

Uvas

Cheese

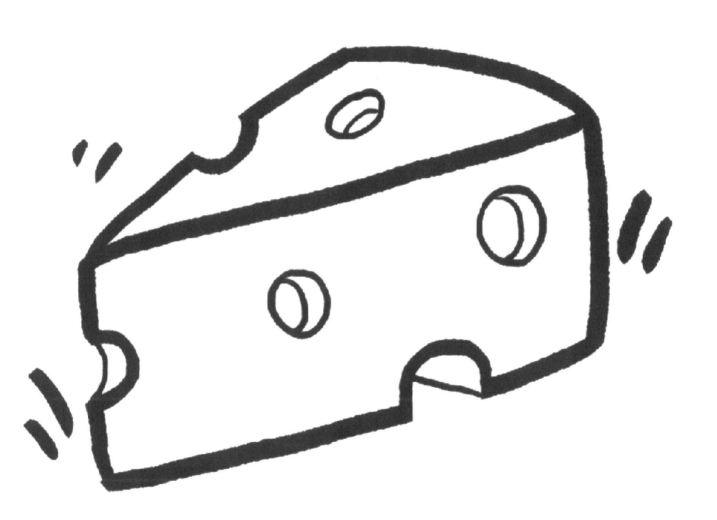

Queso

Milk

Leche

Bread

Pan

Ice Cream

Helado

Cake

Pastel

Cherry

Cereza

Water

Agua

Cow

Vaca

Fish

Pez

Dog

Perro

Bear

Oso

Bird

Pájaro

Zebra

Cebra

Bunny

Conejito

Lion

León

Whale

Ballena

Elephant

Elefante

Owl

Búho

Monkey

Mono

Mouse

Ratón

Horse

Caballo

Cat

Gato

Pig

Cerdo

Circle

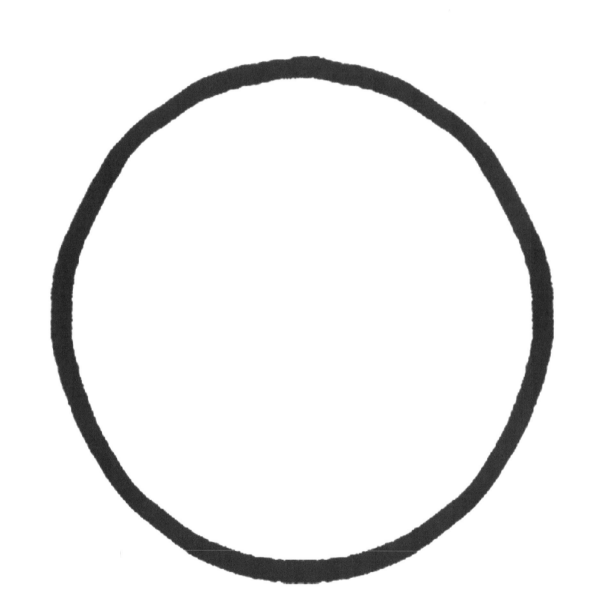

Circulo

Square

Cuadrado

Triangle

Triángulo

Heart

Corazón

Star

Estrella

Moon

Luna

Pants

Pantalones

Shoes

Zapatos

Socks

Calcetines

Shirt

Camisa

Door

Puerta

Chair

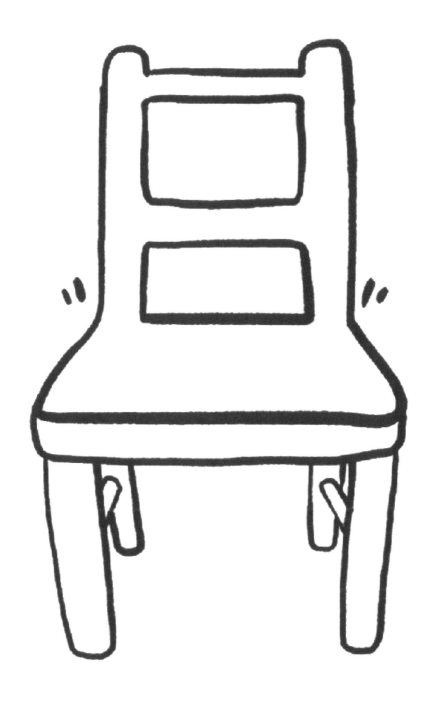

Silla

Book

Libro

Table

Mesa

Bed

Cama

Plate

Plato

Clock

Reloj

Mug

Tazón

Pen

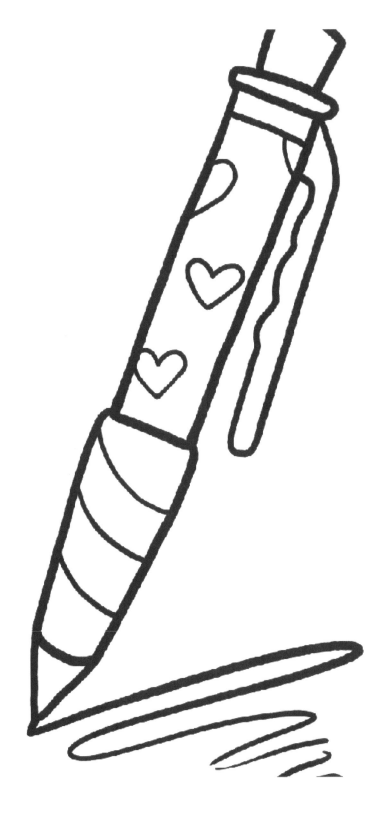

Bolígrafo

Toys

Juguetes

Doll

Muñeca

Ball

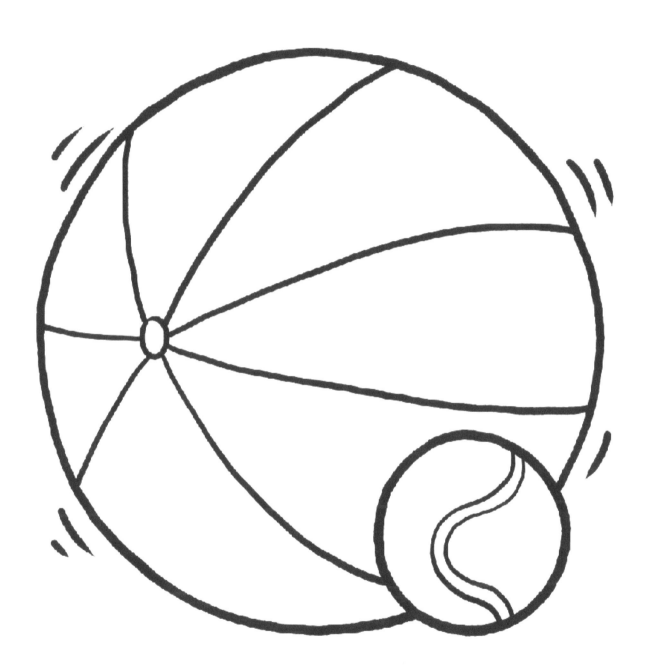

Bola

House

Casa

Tree

Árbol

Flower

Flor

Sun

Sol

Light Stop

Semáforo

Trycicle

Triciclo

Car

Carro

Train

Tren

Airplane

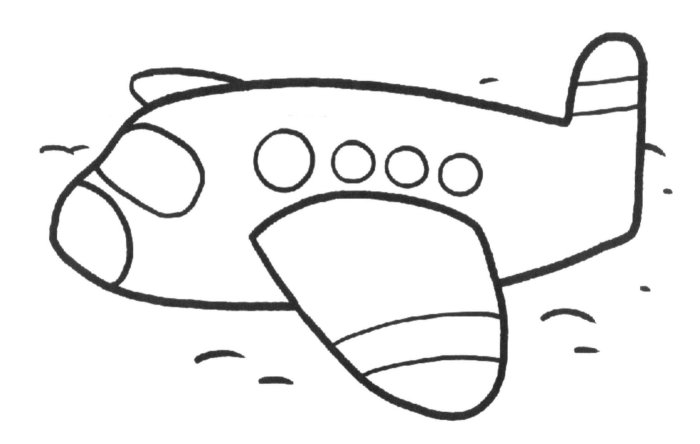

Avión

Bicycle

Bicicleta

Truck

Camión

Boat

Bote

CPSIA information can be obtained
at www.ICGtesting.com
Printed in the USA
LVHW070035020420
651970LV00011B/273